# The Darling Buds of May

*Mr Charlton woke up late the next morning with wild dogs screaming inside his head. But he didn't know if it was his head. And what was he doing lying on a table in a pink shirt and pink trousers?*

It is spring and everything is perfect for Ma and Pa Larkin. True, their oldest daughter, Mariette, is going to have a baby. She doesn't know who the father is, so she needs one, quickly. But they'll think of something. Life is full of surprises – like Mr Charlton, the young man from the Tax Office, when he comes to the Larkins' house . . .

Herbert Ernest Bates (1905–74) was born in Northamptonshire in England. When he was a young man he worked on a local newspaper, then sold his first book at the age of twenty-one.

He always understood the ordinary English people, who lived from the land, and loved to write about them. His stories about the life-loving Larkin family began in 1958 with *The Darling Buds of May*. The books were much less serious than his earlier work and some people didn't like them. But when *The Darling Buds of May* started on British television in 1990 millions of people loved his stories of the wild Larkins.

OTHER TITLES IN THE SERIES

# The Darling Buds of May

## H. E. BATES

Level 3

Retold by David Wharry
Series Editor: Derek Strange

PENGUIN BOOKS

PENGUIN BOOKS

Published by the Penguin Group
Penguin Books Ltd, 27 Wrights Lane, London W8 5TZ, England
Penguin Books USA Inc., 375 Hudson Street, New York, New York 10014, USA
Penguin Books Australia Ltd, Ringwood, Victoria, Australia
Penguin Books Canada Ltd, 10 Alcorn Avenue, Toronto, Ontario, Canada M4V 3B2
Penguin Books (NZ) Ltd, 182–190 Wairau Road, Auckland 10, New Zealand

Penguin Books Ltd, Registered Offices: Harmondsworth, Middlesex, England

*The Darling Buds of May* first published by Michael Joseph 1958
Published in Penguin Books 1961
This adaptation published by Penguin Books 1995
10 9 8 7 6 5 4 3 2 1

Illustrations by Kay Dixey

Printed in England by Clays Ltd, St Ives plc
Set in 11/14pt Lasercomp Bembo by
Datix International Limited, Bungay, Suffolk

## To the teacher:

In addition to all the language forms of Levels One and Three, which are used again at this level of the series, the main verb forms and tenses used at Level Three are:

- past continuous verbs, present perfect simple verbs, conditional clauses (using the 'first' or 'open future' conditional), question tags and further common phrasal verbs
- modal verbs: *have (got) to* and *don't have to* (to express obligation), *need to* and *needn't* (to express necessity), *could* and *was able to* (to describe past ability), *could* and *would* (in offers and polite requests for help), and *shall* (for future plans, offers and suggestions).

Also used are:

- relative pronouns: *who*, *that* and *which* (in defining clauses)
- conjunctions: *if* and *since* (for time or reason), so *that* (for purpose or result) and *while*
- indirect speech (questions)
- participle clauses.

Specific attention is paid to vocabulary development in the Vocabulary Work exercises at the end of the book. These exercises are aimed at training students to enlarge their vocabulary systematically through intelligent reading and effective use of a dictionary.

## To the student:

Dictionary Words:

- When you read this book, you will find that some words are in darker black ink than the others on the page. Look them up in your dictionary, if you do not already know them, or try to guess the meaning of the words first, without a dictionary.

## CHAPTER ONE

Laughing, Pop Larkin gave each of the children an ice-cream and climbed up behind the wheel, still laughing. The bright blue lorry shone in the strong May sun. All along the road, fruit-trees were in flower. Ma, sitting next to Pop, was laughing too. She shook like a great big **jelly**, the sun dancing in her dark eyes and hair. 'Are you children all right?' Pop shouted.

'Yes!' shouted Zinnia, Petunia, Primrose, Victoria and Montgomery.

'I don't hear Mariette,' Pop shouted. 'Has she fallen off?'

'I'm here, Pop,' replied Mariette, the oldest.

Pop pushed Ma. 'Move over a bit, will you, Ma? I can't drive like this.' Ma moved away a little. Pop, a small man with quick eyes, wasn't half her size. 'Perfect!' he said. 'No — wait. Where's my money?'

'In your jacket pocket, with the chocolates,' Ma said, her mouth full of ice-cream.

His hand went in quickly and came out full of chocolates and paper, perhaps a hundred pounds. He threw the chocolates into the back of the lorry and drove away.

'Look at that, everyone!' he shouted as they went past a field of **strawberries**. 'They're almost ready for **picking**.'

'Hooray!' shouted everyone. Only Mariette was silent.

Strawberry-picking began in June, followed by all the other sorts of fruit. When the apples were finished in October, potatoes began. A big family could **earn** as much as fifteen pounds a day.

'What's wrong with Mariette, Ma?' Pop said.

'She's thinking, probably,' Ma said.

'Thinking? What's she got to think about?'

1

'She's going to have a baby.'

'Oh, really?' Pop said. He looked at Ma. She didn't seem to be worried either. 'Perfect. Very good. Who's the father?'

'She thinks it's either that Charles or the boy who worked on the railway. One's married and the other went to work in Egypt.'

'Oh, well, we'll think of something. Let's stop for a beer.'

Ma took another chocolate. Her fingers were like fat little sausages. 'No,' she said. 'Let's go home – we're having fish for dinner.'

'Perfect,' said Pop.

They arrived at the farm ten minutes later. 'Home looks perfect, doesn't it, Ma?' Pop said, driving slowly through the crowd of chickens and **geese**. The birds ran away behind one of the mountains of **scrap** metal.

'It looks wonderful, it always does,' Ma said.

Pop kissed the kids one after the other when they jumped down. Mariette, in riding-trousers and a yellow blouse, was last. Looking at her perfect young body, he remembered how Ma looked exactly like her once. Pop could see that she was worried.

'It's all right, Pop,' she said, 'I don't need any help.'

She walked away and Pop noticed a man standing by the house. He was young, white-faced, wore glasses and looked very unsure of himself. 'Mr Sydney Larkin?' he said shyly.

'That's me,' Pop said. 'Perfect weather, isn't it?'

'I'm from the **Tax** Office,' said the man.

'Really? Are you sure you've come to the right place?'

Looking more uncomfortable, he showed Pop a yellow paper. 'Mr Larkin, did you get a paper like this last year?'

'Paper?' said Pop.

'Like this one. It asks you how much money you earned.'

Pop started laughing. Ma came past with two shopping-bags full of food. 'Ma,' he said, 'this man wants to know how much money we earned last year.'

Ma laughed. 'Money we *lost*, he means, doesn't he? Hey, Pop, hurry up. Dinner's cooking.'

'We don't earn any money,' Pop said, pointing at the farm around him. 'Anybody can see that.'

'We sent you a paper like this three times,' the man said.

'Well, if you did, we never saw it,' Ma replied. 'We haven't got time. We've got geese, chickens, horses, children to look after. All those mouths have to eat, you know.'

'And I have to eat too,' Pop said. 'Would you like to stay for dinner, Mr –?'

The young man didn't reply. He was watching Mariette walking towards them. Looking at her made him feel strange inside. He wasn't sure if he was dreaming or not.

'My oldest daughter,' Pop said. 'She loves riding. Mariette, I think this young man wants to meet you. Do you like horses, Mr –?'

'Charlton,' said the young man, unable to take his eyes off the shapes inside Mariette's yellow blouse. His mouth felt suddenly dry.

'Mr Charlton, meet Mariette. She likes riding horses. "Who's that nice young man?" she said when she saw you.'

When Mariette smiled at Mr Charlton, his legs felt suddenly very weak. Her mouth was like a bright red strawberry.

Mr Charlton pulled his eyes away from her. 'Mr Larkin, this yellow paper, I –'

'Come in and have some fish, Mr Charlton,' Pop said. 'It's no trouble, honestly. Do you like fish – nice fresh fish?'

'I'm sorry, but I don't like fish, Mr Larkin, I –'

'A cup of tea then, or a beer, or coffee. Anything you want.'

'I – I'm not really hungry,' he said, looking helplessly at her blouse again. His head seemed to be turning round and round. She smiled at him and he followed her quietly to the house.

3

Pop threw up his arms to the wonderful day. 'Perfect, Mr Charlton, isn't it? And I've got a beautiful home here, haven't I?'

In the living-room the television was on, giving the nine faces round the table a purple colour. The Larkins each had a mountain of fish on their plates. On the table there were more mountains, of ice-cream, butter, bread, tomatoes, bananas, oranges, cakes.

'Have what you like, Mr Charlton,' Pop said. 'Tea? Beer? Wine? If it's not on the table, ask for it! Do you like sausages?'

'I – er . . .'

'Ma,' Pop shouted into the kitchen. 'He likes sausages.'

Ma came in and sat down. 'There's something wrong with that new television, Pop. The picture has gone dark again.'

Mr Charlton, sitting next to Mariette, put the yellow paper on the table. 'Mr Larkin, perhaps I could help you with this?'

'Yes, all right,' said Pop. 'Write it all down for me, if you like.'

Mr Charlton began writing. 'Full name: Mr Sydney Larkin. Job: buyer and seller of scrap metal.'

'What?' Ma said sharply. 'He's got land. He's a farmer. Montgomery, change that television.'

When she took the butter, Mariette's arm touched Mr Charlton's. Hot and cold ran up his back when he felt her skin against his.

'Home-made butter from our farm, Mr Charlton,' Ma said. 'Mariette, are those sausages cooked yet?' Seconds later, Mariette put a plate of sausages and eggs down in front of Mr Charlton. 'Home-made,' Ma said. 'Do you like sausages?'

'I, er – yes, I do.' Mr Charlton pulled the paper out from under the plate. 'Six children, Mr Larkin? Is that right? No more?'

'Not yet,' said Pop, and laughed. 'Give us time.' He gave

*Mr Charlton pulled the paper out from under the plate.*
*'Six children, Mr Larkin? Is that right? No more?'*

Mr Charlton a knife and fork. 'You look like you don't eat enough.'

'It's not always easy – I'm not a very good cook.' When he said this he felt something smooth pressing against the inside of his leg. Could it be *her*? She smiled and again he felt something wonderfully smooth touch him inside his leg. Shaking, he looked down and saw a white neck. There were geese under the table.

Montgomery, bringing another television, passed a large piece of furniture like a ship. 'Look out for the **cocktail** cupboard!' Ma shouted.

Trying hard not to think of the wonderful smoothness, Mr Charlton said, 'Now, Mr Larkin, if you could tell me how much –'

'Come on, young man, eat up. Ma doesn't like to see food wasted.'

'Mr Larkin, we need an idea of how much money you earned.'

'Idea?' Pop said. 'I'm not very good at numbers, but we're lucky if we see five pounds in a week, aren't we, Ma?'

Ma took more ice-cream. 'It's not often we have that much.'

Mr Charlton thought. 'Five hundred pounds a year, shall we say?'

Pop laughed. 'There are a hundred weeks in a year now, Ma!' Now, Mr Charlton, I'll ask *you*. How much do you earn, then?'

'Oh, my job isn't very well paid at all, Mr Larkin.'

'But it's a nice, safe office job. Are you happy in it?'

Mr Charlton didn't look very happy about anything.

'You look like you need a few days in the country, young man,' Ma said. 'You haven't got enough colour.'

'I hope your eggs are all right,' Mariette said.

'Do you like goose, Mr Charlton?' Pop said. 'We're having goose for lunch on Sunday.'

Mr Charlton couldn't decide if Pop was asking him to lunch or not. Mariette's warm, dark smile seemed to say yes.

Pop started laughing. 'I think those poor geese heard what I said, Ma. They've just run out of the door.'

'Mariette,' said Ma, 'why don't you and Mr Charlton go and listen to the birds in the forest? It'll be nice and quiet there.'

'Yes!' said Mariette, jumping up. 'We can ride there.'

'I – er . . . Why don't we walk?'

'All right. I'll go and put on a dress. It's too hot for trousers.'

The children went to look after the chickens. 'Everybody has to work here, Mr Charlton,' Pop said. 'Otherwise how would we eat?'

Watching the young man eat, Ma said, 'You look tired, Mr Charlton. Are you taking your holiday soon?'

'I – er . . . No, I'm not.'

'Strawberry-picking is the best holiday in the world, isn't it, Pa?'

'Yes,' he said. 'And it doesn't cost anything – you earn money! Why don't you come with us? It'll be good for you.'

Mr Charlton stood up when Mariette came in, bright and fresh in a low-cut green dress. Again he asked himself if she was real or not.

'Are you sure you'll be warm enough in that?' Ma said.

'I love feeling the wind against me,' Mariette replied.

Mr Charlton thought of her in the quiet shadows of the forest, the wind, as smooth as the goose's neck, playing on her long brown legs. 'Are you coming, Mr Charlton?' she said.

'I – er. Er . . . Mr Larkin, the yellow paper, I . . .'

'We'll finish it on Sunday. See you on Sunday, Mr Charlton.'

Watching them walk away past the mountains of scrap

metal, Pop said, 'I'll get more wine for Sunday, so we can drink to the good news. But you know, Ma, it'll break my heart to see my little Mariette leave.'

## CHAPTER TWO

Mariette, with a bunch of flowers, and Mr Charlton, carefully carrying two wild bird's eggs, returned only an hour later. Pop was outside looking at the pigs. 'I think we'll kill two,' he said. 'You're just in time for tea, Mr Charlton. Did you hear any birds?'

'I thought we just had tea,' Mr Charlton said.

'That was dinner,' Mariette said.

'I must catch my bus home.'

'Mariette can drive you home later,' Pop said. 'And she'll drive you here on Sunday.'

'I don't think I'll have time to come again, Mr Larkin. Now, could we go into the question of tax before I leave?'

'Tea first,' Pop said.

'Mr Larkin, if you don't reply to this paper, my office will want to know why.'

'And Ma will be angry if you don't come in and have tea.'

'We're having steak,' Mariette said. 'I'll go and help Ma.'

Inside, Mariette put the wild flowers in water while Ma cooked.

'How did it go with Mr Charlton, dear?'

'Slow. We talked about horses. He's very, very shy.'

Ma shook her head sadly. 'You'll have to find something a bit more exciting to talk about. And he's thin. He needs to eat more. I'll give him a nice fat piece of steak.'

Montgomery, Pop and Mr Charlton came in and sat at the table with the others. On the television, a boring-looking woman was talking about family planning.

'Montgomery's heard that strawberry-picking begins on Monday at Benacre Farm,' Pop said. He watched Ma put the biggest steak on Mr Charlton's plate and smiled. 'And give the young man a nice big cup of tea, Primrose.' He went to the cocktail cupboard and took out a bottle of whisky. 'Have a bit of "milk" in your tea, Mr Charlton.'

'No, please!' Mr Charlton said, but Pop was already **filling** his cup. Mariette sat down and he was sure, this time, that her leg touched his.

'We want to know what your other name is, Mr Charlton,' Pop said. 'We can't go on calling you "Mr", can we?'

'Cedric,' he said, and saw everyone laugh. Ma couldn't stop. Pop hit her hard on the back.

'Don't worry about her, er – Charlie, she's eaten too much.'

Mr Charlton looked shyly at Mariette. She smiled at him with dark, silent eyes and he felt quite afraid.

'You won't be angry if we call you Charlie, will you?' Pop said.

'Er, no. Mr Larkin, I'm sorry, but I must catch that bus.'

'There's no bus on Friday evenings,' Ma said.

'Then I must start walking – it's eight miles to Fordington.'

'No, you mustn't. You can stay the night, Charlie,' Pop said.

'We'll make a bed on the table in the other room,' Ma said.

'And tomorrow's Saturday,' Mariette said. 'We can go riding. You can have some of my clothes to sleep in.'

'No, I'm sorry, I really must go,' Mr Charlton said. He drank his tea quickly and closed his eyes while the whisky burnt through him. Primrose gave him more tea. Pop put in more whisky.

'A few days' strawberry-picking is what you need,' Ma said, opening four very expensive tins of foreign fruit.

On the television, a woman was standing by a large house

in a park. 'We're going to visit Fanshawe Castle, the home of Lord and Lady Peele. We will begin with the famous library.'

'Oh, look at the library!' said Ma. 'It's wonderful.'

'What's that all over the walls?' Pop said.

'Perhaps it's books,' Ma said. 'And look at that furniture.'

'Lady Peele couldn't pay her taxes,' Mr Charlton said, feeling the whisky going to his head. 'She'll have to sell that house to pay – and you too, Mr Larkin. Your tax –'

Mariette took his hand. 'Come on, Mr Charlton, let's go and find those nightclothes for you.'

He didn't know why he couldn't say no. She took him upstairs.

Much later, Pop, Ma and Mariette were trying to teach Mr Charlton 'crib', their favourite game of cards. 'It's easy,' Pop said. 'All you have to do is use your head and know how to count. You tax people are good at numbers, aren't you?'

'I work with a very different kind of numbers, Mr Larkin.'

Pop laughed. 'Believe me, Charlie, numbers are all the same. Now, you just look at those cards and use your head.'

Mr Charlton's head was beginning to feel terrible – too many of those teas, and how many beers? He couldn't remember.

Pop stood up suddenly. 'I'm going to mix a cocktail.'

'It's so hot in here,' said Mariette. 'I think I'll go outside, Mr Charlton. Why don't you come too?'

'After he's had his cocktail,' Pop said, looking in his cocktail book. 'Ah, here's one we haven't had. "Rolls-Royce"*: a quarter whisky, a quarter wine, a quarter orange . . . This'll blow our heads off!' He proudly opened the ship. 'Do you like our new cocktail cupboard, Mr Charlton? It cost £150.'

* 'Rolls-Royce' is usually the name of an expensive and comfortable British car.

Pop mixed the cocktails, drank a whole glass, opened his eyes wide for a few seconds and said, 'Perfect! This'll grow hair on you, Charlie. Come on, drink up.'

Mr Charlton drank and felt a white-hot knife cut down through him. **Fireworks** started going off inside his head.

'It really gets under your skin, doesn't it?' Pop said. 'Let's have another one. And Ma, let's have something to eat with it.'

Mr Charlton started laughing, he didn't know why. Pop hit him hard on the back. 'We feel you're one of the family, Charlie.'

Two Rolls-Royces later, Mr Charlton started laughing again. Everyone laughed with him and he looked into Mariette's eyes. For the first time he wasn't afraid. 'Your eyes are so beautiful and dark,' he said across the table. 'What colour are they?'

'Come and sit here and you'll see,' she replied.

He went and sat down next to Mariette and noticed that Pop was gone. Ma screamed. 'I'm here, under Ma!' Pop said. 'Why don't you ask Mariette to sit on you?'

Mariette didn't wait for him to ask. She sat on his knees and he felt her legs, wonderfully smooth like the goose's neck.

'That's enough Rolls-Royces,' Pop said. 'I'll make a Driver. Every Rolls-Royce has to have a Driver, doesn't it, Charlie?'

Mariette pulled his arms round her, under her **breasts**. 'You're my smooth, sweet little goose,' he said in her ear.

Two Drivers later, Mr Charlton stood up and said in a loud voice, 'Pop, we must think of a cocktail called "Mariette".'

'And you must be the first to taste it,' Mariette said.

Some time later, it seemed to Mr Charlton that he was on his knees in a dark room, kissing a leg. 'Go on, get up,' the leg said. 'I'll take your shirt off.' Then everything went black.

11

Upstairs, Pop sat in bed smoking a cigar, watching Ma pull her red nightdress down over her great mountains and shadowy valleys. She looked like a great big strawberry.

'Ma,' he said, 'I'm worried about Mr Charlton. I'm not sure the young man has it in him.'

'No, he hasn't – not yet. But don't worry. Mariette will work on him. She's probably working on him right now.'

## CHAPTER THREE

Mr Charlton woke up late the next morning with wild dogs screaming inside his head. But he didn't know if it was *his* head. And what was he doing lying on a table in a pink shirt and pink trousers?

A few uncomfortable minutes later he dressed and walked carefully to the kitchen. Ma was singing, cooking sausages and eggs. He had to look away from the food. When he took a chair, his hand was shaking.

'Mariette's gone riding,' Ma said. 'Pop will come in for his second breakfast in a minute. Do you want two eggs or three?'

Seconds later something hit Mr Charlton hard between the shoulders. 'Perfect morning. How's my friend the tax-man?' Pop sat down. 'I'm taking two pigs to the meat factory this morning, Charlie. You can come with me if you want.'

'I think I shall have to go home, Mr Larkin.'

Ma put down a plate of sausages and eggs in front of him. He shut his eyes. Opening them again, he saw Mariette smiling at him in a yellow blouse and riding-trousers.

'Hello, bright eyes,' she said, and laughed. 'Honestly, Mr Charlton, you were so funny last night. You tried to kiss the table leg! And I don't know how we put my trousers on you.'

*What was he doing lying on a table in a pink shirt and pink trousers?*

The Larkins all laughed. Pop went to the ship-cupboard and took out bottles. 'Charlie, my boy, you need a Larkin Special.'

'After breakfast we can go down to the river,' Mariette said. 'I'll show you our boat, if you like.'

'Boat?' Mr Charlton said, remembering the tax paper.

'Someone gave it to us – instead of money,' Pop said quickly. 'Now, drink this and you'll soon feel perfect.'

Mr Charlton's stomach turned over when he saw the drink. It had an egg in it. Mariette smiled sweetly at him. He wanted to hold her in his arms. He put the glass to his lips and drank.

'I've got business with those pigs,' Pop said. 'Bye-bye, every-one.'

After Pop left, Mr Charlton sat silently for some time. Slowly the storm left his head. He began to hear the birds singing outside.

'You're not really going home today, are you?' Mariette said.

He thought of the little room he lived in, of his boring office.

'Let's get some air,' she said. He followed her outside into the sun. The sky was deep blue. 'How do you feel?' she said.

'Perfect,' he said, and smiled at her.


## CHAPTER FOUR

At midday on Sunday, Mr Charlton and Mariette were putting knives and forks on the table under the apple tree when Pop drove up to the house in a Rolls-Royce. 'It's ours,' he shouted, getting out proudly. Everybody ran to touch the car's shining body. Ma couldn't believe her eyes.

'Did it belong to a king?' said Zinnia.

14

*Mr Charlton and Mariette were putting knives and forks on the table under the apple tree when Pop drove up to the house in a Rolls-Royce.*

'I don't know – maybe,' Pop said. 'Look inside, there are special cups for flowers, and there's a telephone for speaking to the driver. Come on, there's room for the whole family.'

Ma got in. 'I feel like a queen – oh, I haven't got my hat on!'

'Take us for a ride, Driver,' the children all shouted.

'No!' Ma said. 'Those geese'll burn if we do.' Getting out, she touched the paint again; it was like a mirror. 'Every time we go out I want flowers in those cups,' she said.

Mariette and Mr Charlton went to finish the table. 'Charlie?' Pop called. 'Put that wine on ice, will you?' He noticed a tall, straight man, like a piece of dry grass, coming towards them.

'Ah, Larkin, there you are.'

'Brigadier!' Pop said, and shook the old soldier's hand.

'It isn't yours?' he said, looking at the car with a dry smile.

'I just got it,' Pop said.

'I don't believe it,' the Brigadier said. 'An expensive plaything.'

Pop laughed. 'Oh, don't worry, if it's too expensive to keep, I'll sell it. A drink, Brigadier?'

In the sitting-room, the Brigadier sat with his glass on his left knee, over a hole in his trousers there. He always wore the same old suit, mended in several places. 'Larkin,' he said, 'there was a meeting in the village on Friday about the Horse Show, and I'm sorry to say that we can't use our usual field this year. We were –'

'Nothing to worry about,' Pop said. 'You can use mine.'

'Larkin, thank you! We'll never be able to thank you enough.'

Pop gave him another whisky. Ma came in. Like Pop, she liked the Brigadier. They felt sorry for the poor man, living alone with that terrible sister who never gave him enough to eat.

'You'll stay to lunch, won't you?' she said.

The smell of the geese cooking was bringing water to the Brigadier's mouth. 'Oh, no, thanks, I'll eat something at the pub.'

'You won't, Brigadier!' Ma said. 'Pop, come and lift the goose out of the oven.'

In the kitchen, they saw Mariette and Mr Charlton sitting at the table outside, on opposite sides of it. Mr Charlton was reading the newspaper.

'Look at that!' Ma said. 'What's wrong with them?'

Pop shook his head sadly. 'Let's hope he's more interested in her on the boat this afternoon. There are some nice quiet places up the river, remember?' He took Ma in his arms and kissed her on her big soft mouth. He often felt excited in the kitchen – it was the smell of the food. Slowly his hand came up her leg, pulling up her dress.

She started laughing. 'Stop it – it's either me or dinner.'

Half an hour later everyone was sitting under the apple tree. Pop was cutting up the geese, Mariette was putting vegetables on each plate and Mr Charlton was filling glasses with wine.

The Brigadier got up and lifted his glass to Ma. 'To the cook!'

'Look, the Brigadier's got holes in his socks,' Victoria said.

'You be quiet!' Ma said. 'Now Pop, tell everyone.'

When Pop proudly told them about the Horse Show, Mariette screamed, jumped up and ran and kissed him on the lips.

'Thank the Brigadier, not me,' Pop said. 'It was his idea.'

She ran and kissed the Brigadier, then said, 'Oh, Mr Charlton, I'm so happy, I think I'll kiss you too!' Everyone laughed. He was shaking and red in the face when her lips touched his.

'It's time to go and get the ice-cream from the kitchen,' she said into his ear. But sadly Mr Charlton didn't see this perfect way of having another kiss. The more she liked him, the more she felt sorry for him. Perhaps making love to her in the long grass would help him. She wanted to help him.

After the ice-cream Mr Charlton missed a second kiss when Mariette went into the house to make tea. Ma couldn't understand what was wrong with the young man.

'You'll get a visit from Edith Pilchester soon,' the Brigadier said to Pop. 'She's secretary for the Horse Show this year.'

'Oh, I love old Edith,' Pop said. 'She likes a good laugh.'

Watching Mariette return with the tea, the Brigadier said, 'She's grown into a beautiful young woman, Mrs Larkin.'

'I'm glad somebody thinks so,' Ma said loudly, looking hard at Mr Charlton.

As Pop put whisky into everybody's tea he suddenly thought of something. 'I've got a perfect idea to end the Horse Show, Brigadier,' he said. 'Fireworks. What do you think?'

The Brigadier, already half asleep, didn't reply. And Ma, her eyes closed, was falling to one side.

Pop put a cigar next to the Brigadier's cup. He was a nice man – not like some people in the village. They thought they were better than him and Ma. That was why they sent the Brigadier to ask about the field. But he liked Edith Pilchester. Perhaps he would put a firework under her skirt – just to see what happened. 'Look at that beautiful sky, Charlie' he said. 'I don't know how people can work in offices. Cigar?'

'I think we're going now,' Mariette said. 'Aren't we, Mr Charlton?'

As they went into the field Mariette took Mr Charlton's hand. Then she kicked off her shoes and ran. Seeing her brown feet in the long grass excited him. Seconds later he was running too.

That evening, Pop said, 'Charlie, me and Ma think you

*Mariette kicked off her shoes and ran. Seconds later Mr Charlton was running too.*

don't look very well. You've got no colour. And Mariette says your hands are hot – that's bad. A rest is what you need, my boy. Why don't you telephone the office tomorrow and say you're sick?'

'You can stay here next week, love,' Mariette said.

He immediately said no, he couldn't. But later, on the dark stairs, Mariette's lips helped him to begin to think about staying.

## CHAPTER FIVE

Next morning, eating a mountainous breakfast with Pop, Mr Charlton said, 'I don't know what to tell the office when I telephone.'

'You've got a bad back, haven't you?' Pop said.

They drove through the sweet-smelling fields and the children all sang. When they arrived at the strawberry fields at eight o'clock, about thirty women were already working. Mr Charlton's breakfast was doing strange things to his stomach. He felt sick. And it was already hot.

'You can eat all the strawberries you want,' Mariette said.

He found that he was very slow at picking. After half an hour Mariette said, 'I'm hungry. Come and have something to eat with me.'

When he said he wasn't feeling very well, Ma said, 'You see, we told you. Now come on, let's go and **weigh** our strawberries. I can see Pop waving. He's with the boss in the weighing-tent.'

'This is Charlie boy,' Pop said to the boss when they arrived. 'He knows how to use his head.'

'Then he's the person I'm looking for,' the boss said. 'I need someone to weigh the strawberries and write everything down.'

'I've got to go and see a man about some scrap metal, Charlie boy,' Pop said. 'I'll come back at about five.'

The boss explained everything, and before he left with Pop he said, 'Be careful. Some of those women will try things behind your back.'

Mr Charlton sat down, feeling better. It wasn't so hot in the tent. Soon women started coming in with their strawberries. They all wanted to laugh and have a good time and several of them tried to make him make mistakes about the weight. He soon learned that he had to keep his eyes open. The whole Larkin family came in eating chocolate. Ma left some on his desk for him.

Later, when it was quiet, a very pretty, very well-built girl came into the tent. She wore jeans and a blouse that showed perfectly her full, young breasts, underneath.

'Pauline Jackson, twenty-four boxes,' she said almost sleepily. Her tongue played with her perfect white teeth while he wrote her name. 'Is it true your name is Cedric?'

He felt his face going red. 'No. Ask the Larkins, ask Mariette. They call me Charlie.'

'Oh, *she* knows you, does she?' She took a strawberry, ate it. 'Don't you like strawberries? I haven't seen you eating any.'

'I haven't got time. I've got too many other things to do.'

'Like what?' She came closer. Her half-open blouse, showing the deep valley between her breasts, was in front of his nose now. She took the chocolate. 'Can I have some, Charlie?' she asked softly.

Mariette came in, her eyes like dark fire. Pauline, eating the chocolate, looked at her calmly and said, 'See you later, Charlie.' She gave him a long smile and left.

Mariette put her boxes down angrily. 'That Pauline is a dirty cat!' she said loudly, and turned to leave.

'Don't go,' Mr Charlton said. 'Please, I want to talk to you.'

21

She thought for a second or two. 'I've got to calm down, Charlie. If you want me, I'll be over there under the trees.'

But Mr Charlton didn't have time.

By the middle of the afternoon it was so hot that women were taking off their blouses and working in their **brassières**, all shapes, sizes and colours. Mr Charlton was busy counting when Pauline, now without her blouse, came in again. She came up to him. Her breasts were so full inside her black brassière that he thought they would jump out at him. His heart began to jump up and down.

'I can drive you back to Fordington if you want,' she said. 'Maybe we can go for a swim together, too.' Her breasts, like fruit in their cups, came nearer. 'Just tell me when you're ready to go.'

Later, he was weighing a woman's boxes of strawberries when suddenly he heard screaming and shouting outside. He saw a crowd. The woman ran outside. 'Come and watch! It's a fight!' she said. 'Ooh! It's Mariette and Pauline!'

Mr Charlton ran out and saw the two girls fighting like wild cats. Ma was shouting excitedly. He saw blood in their hair, on their faces, but running closer he saw that it was only strawberry juice. He pushed through the crowd and pulled Mariette away from Pauline. 'Stop it!' he shouted, 'Before you kill yourselves! What are you two fighting for?'

'Don't you know, Charlie boy?' Ma said.

Everyone started laughing. Looking round, he realized that all the women were laughing at him. Then he knew: Mariette was fighting for *him*!

Driving home that evening, he couldn't stop smiling at Mariette, feeling more and more proud of her.

'How did it go, Charlie?' Pop asked later, giving him a beer.

'Those pickers earn a lot of money, don't they? Do they pay tax?'

*Mr Charlton ran out and saw the two girls fighting like wild cats.*
*He pushed through the crowd and pulled Mariette away from*
*Pauline.*

Pop put a hand on Mr Charlton's shoulder. 'Use your head, Charlie boy. Who's going to do any picking if they have to pay tax? And somebody has to pick those strawberries, don't they?'

Mariette came in, washed and smiling in a fresh green dress.

'Why don't you take Mariette down to the river before dinner?' Pop said. 'I'm going to cut the grass in that field tomorrow.'

## CHAPTER SIX

When Pop arrived home next evening Miss Pilchester was waiting for him. She was about forty, always wore thick grey clothes and had a noticeable moustache. 'Isn't it terrible,' she said with a sad smile. Pop didn't know what was terrible and didn't ask: she always said everything was terrible.

She went everywhere by bicycle. Since the war she hadn't enough money for a car because of all the terrible taxes and the terrible prices. The people who went fruit-picking earned much more money than she did with her chickens. It was all really terrible.

She looked at the freshly cut field. 'A beautiful field, Larkin.'

Pop laughed. 'I'm always happy to be useful.'

She laughed too, remembering the time they kissed once, during a game at a Christmas party.

He asked her in for a drink. In the kitchen, Ma was busy cutting up a mountain of meat. 'The pigs came back from the factory,' she said. 'And Doctor Leagrave is in the sitting-room.'

Leagrave, a heavy, red-nosed man, looked tired. 'I'm always busy in hot weather,' he said. 'Everybody suddenly gets ill.'

'Laziness,' Pop said sadly. 'People are afraid of hard work.'

Miss Pilchester thought it was terrible. Everyone agreed.

'The Doctor's here to see a friend of ours with a bad back,' Pop said. He found Mr Charlton and the three men went upstairs to Mariette's bedroom. Mr Charlton, red-faced from a second day in the sun, took off his shirt and lay down. The smell of the bed – her smell – excited him. Leagrave touched his back once with his finger and said he needed two weeks' rest. Pop told the doctor not to forget to take a nice big piece of **pork** home with him.

Later, after Leagrave left, Pop gave Edith two large pieces of pork too, and said he wanted to drive her home in his new car.

'You mean the Rolls-Royce!' she said. 'It's not *yours*, is it?'

'You can sit in the back and talk to me on the telephone.'

'No,' she replied quickly. 'I'll sit in the front with you.'

Later, while they drove along, Pop's hand went slowly down and held her knee. She liked this a lot and kept giving him bright little smiles.

She lived in a little house on a small, half-wild piece of land she called a garden. The house was untidy inside too and smelled of unwashed dishes. 'Sit down,' she said, taking an old newspaper, an old grey brassière and a dead chicken from a chair.

'No television?' Pop said, watching her fill two glasses with whisky.

'I don't have enough money. I lost it all in the war.'

Pop said how terrible everything was since the war. 'The tax people pick all the fruit of people's hard work,' he said, and did what she was most afraid of: he finished his drink and got up to leave.

'Please, don't go,' she said. Then suddenly she was in his arms. Fire ran through her body as he pushed his tongue between her lips. Afterwards, as Pop was taking air, she said, 'Please, please! Another one!'

Five minutes later nothing seemed quite as terrible. Shaky, but very happy, she waved to Pop when he drove away.

When he arrived home Ma was sitting outside under the stars enjoying a beer.

'Where's Mr Charlton?' Pop said.

'He wrote a letter to the Tax Office. Mariette took him to post it.'

'A letter? It wasn't about us, I hope?'

'Oh, no,' said Ma, unworried. 'It was about him being sick.'

Pop told Ma about how poorly Miss Pilchester lived, and how untidy and dirty her house was. They agreed it was terrible.

'So, did you kiss her?' Ma asked.

'Of course I did.'

'Good,' she said. 'It's what she needs. What was it like?'

'It felt funny kissing somebody with a moustache.'

Ma started laughing like a jelly. 'Come on, I'm waiting.'

Pop sat down on her knees and, pressing against her breasts, he kissed her. A minute later, like a swimmer coming up for air, she said, 'That's enough now. I don't want you to get too tired, do I?'

**CHAPTER SEVEN**

The morning of the Horse Show the Larkins were all up with the birds, busy with different jobs. Later, at breakfast, everyone had sausages, eggs, potatoes and tomatoes. Watching Mariette fill Mr Charlton's cup a second time, Pop said, 'Too much tea isn't good for you, you know. Have a beer with me.'

Mr Charlton's mouth was too full of food to reply. Pop smiled. He liked to see Mr Charlton eat. 'You two look after

*Five minutes later nothing seemed as terrible. Shaky, but very happy, she waved to Pop when he drove away.*

the **donkeys** after breakfast. I've got too much to do and Miss Pilchester will be here at six.'

'Pop borrowed the donkeys,' Mariette said. 'Miss Pilchester didn't like his idea of fireworks, so he thought a donkey **race** was a good idea instead.'

'What time is the cocktail party, Pop?' Mr Charlton asked.

'Ma thinks eight o'clock is perfect.' Neither he nor Ma knew what people ate at cocktail parties. He asked Mr Charlton.

'Oh, *canapés*, *vol-au-vents*, *pistachios*, that sort of thing.'

'What? I've never heard words like that. Not on the radio or on television.'

'They're foreign words, meaning small little things to eat.'

'That won't keep people alive for very long,' Ma said. 'People need sausages and cakes, that sort of thing.'

'And I'll make Rolls-Royces, Drivers, Green Spiders,' Pop said. 'And Fireball. Their hair will fall out with Fireball!'

Mariette and Mr Charlton went to look after the donkeys. As soon as they were round the corner of the house he took her in his arms and kissed her, running his hands over her shoulders and breasts. Yes, he was learning, and Mariette felt so wonderful that it almost hurt.

At ten o'clock, the Brigadier and Pop were helping with the tents when Miss Pilchester arrived at last, four hours late. Immediately she was hurrying everywhere, ordering everyone. Everything was terrible!

The Brigadier looked at his watch. 'I must go home for lunch.'

'Not before you've been to the beer tent with me,' Pop said.

Already the tent was crowded with local people. Pop knew most of them – rich people with long names who thought everything belonged to them.

'How's everybody?' he said loudly, just to see if anybody

*The Brigadier and Pop were helping with the tents when Miss
Pilchester arrived at last, four hours late.*

answered – and of course almost nobody did. They all thought they were above him and Ma. But it didn't matter what they thought.

He went over to Sir George Bluff-Gore, a sad-looking man with yellowish skin. He had a very large house that was much too expensive for him to look after. They talked for a few minutes about horses, then Pop suddenly changed the subject.

'So, when are you going to sell the house, Sir George?' he asked.

Bluff-Gore went white. 'What? Why do you think I want to sell it?'

'Well, you only live in a small part of it, don't you?' Pop replied openly. 'It's got sixty rooms. It's like having a car you never use.'

Bluff-Gore smiled coolly. '*You* weren't thinking of buying it?'

'Of course I was,' Pop said smoothly. 'There's a lot of good scrap in that house: stone, metal, wood, glass. Think about it.'

He left Bluff-Gore looking helplessly at his feet and went outside. Mariette was on her horse; she looked wonderful. Mr Charlton was with her. No more riding for *her* soon, Pop thought.

All afternoon Mr Charlton sat happily watching Mariette riding and jumping. Ma sat with him, dressed in blue. She was happy too: Mariette looked beautiful, the children were all prettily dressed, and she was too. But where was Pop?

He was behind the beer tent with Miss Pilchester.

'No, Mr Larkin, no!' she was saying. 'You'll never see me ride a donkey.'

'Oh, come on, Edith, they're all young girls of your age.' She smiled. 'Do you remember the other night?'

She felt his fingers on her leg. 'Be careful! Somebody'll see us!'

*Ma was happy: Mariette looked beautiful, the children were all prettily dressed, and she was too. But where was Pop?*

At four-thirty, Montgomery and Mr Charlton rode in the men's donkey race. All the donkeys were so lazy, people had to push them. Jasmine was the only donkey who ran without pushing and Mr Charlton fell off her after only five metres. Kicking and jumping, she ran all the way down to the river for a drink. Mr Charlton and Mariette went to get her back.

At five o'clock, Pop helped Miss Pilchester to climb on to Jasmine. 'Hold on with your knees,' he said.

Looking round, she was surprised to see all the other riders were young girls. The donkey felt very rough and hairy between her legs.

The race began. This time all the donkeys went slowly forward. But not Jasmine. Pop pushed her from behind, but she would not move.

'Oh, this is all so truly terrible,' Miss Pilchester said, seeing everyone laughing at her.

Then suddenly Jasmine jumped forward, knocking Pop to the ground. Holding on hard, Miss Pilchester and Jasmine flew past all the others, past the finish line and straight down to the river.

Jasmine stopped next to a soldier lying with a girl in the grass. The soldier looked up, saw Miss Pilchester and said, 'Why don't you go away – you *and* your sister.'

## CHAPTER EIGHT

By half past eight that evening there were sixty people in the living-room. Ma, like a big blue bird, came towards Pop through the crowd, laughing. 'We didn't ask all these people. But it's nice, isn't it, Pop?'

A silver-haired woman came up to Pop. 'Ah, Lady Bluff-Gore,' he said. 'How nice to see you.'

She smiled, showing very long teeth. 'I hear you said something interesting to my husband today.'

'Yes. It's time that you knocked down that old place of yours.'

Secretly, Lady Bluff-Gore often thought the same thing. She took Pop's arm. 'Can we go and talk somewhere quiet?'

Outside, she said, 'It will be difficult, Mr Larkin. My husband loves the "old place" too much. But I will do my best, and if he does say yes, perhaps we – you and I – can agree to something between ourselves?'

Pop smiled. Women were all the same: clever. She wanted her 5%. 'I understand perfectly, Lady Bluff-Gore,' he said. 'And I'm sure you'll do your best.'

In the crowd inside the house, another hand took his arm. 'And me?' said Miss Pilchester. 'Have you forgotten your promise?'

Another one who wants her 5%, Pop thought. He took her outside, behind the house, and kissed her long and hard.

'Thanks,' she said, looking at him wildly. 'Now, another.'

'Last one,' said Pop, and kissed her again.

'Today has been a wonderfully happy day,' she said when they finished. 'It was the best Horse Show we've ever had.'

People were dancing now. Inside the smoky room another hand took Pop's arm. It belonged to a tall, fair, very beautiful young woman he didn't know. 'I'm having a party next week,' she said. 'I hope you'll come.' She pulled Pop into a dance with her and went on: 'That donkey ride! My dear man, I laughed so much I nearly died.' She looked at him with wonderfully warm eyes. 'I'm Angela Snow – of Elmhurst Valley. We're having our Horse Show in August and I want your donkeys to end it with a laugh.'

'Do you like fireworks?' he asked.

'I love them – specially the ones that go "bang!"'

'I know a cocktail that goes bang. Do you like cocktails?'

'Of course. Do you know how to make a Snake Bite?'

'Oh, yes,' he said. 'Come with me and I'll show you.' He

was beginning to feel very comfortable with this beautiful young stranger. She liked a good laugh.

Ten minutes later the first firework went 'bang!' under Ma. People started screaming, but Ma only laughed like a jelly. Seconds later, Angela Snow put two more under the Brigadier's sister. People ran into the garden, but Pop was already putting a match to some more fireworks outside. Soon they were going 'bang!' all over the place. Pop put one under Miss Pilchester.

Bang!

She started screaming. 'My skirt is burning! I'm on fire!'

'You always were a hot one!' Pop said, laughing so much that it hurt. Happy as a little boy, he raced everywhere putting fireworks under people.

In the middle of all this, Mr Charlton came up to him. 'Pop, Ma says I can marry Mariette if you agree.'

'Perfect!' Pop shouted, putting a match to the last, biggest firework he had. 'Of course I agree.'

Whoooosh-boom! went the firework, raining silver and gold, and seconds later Pop was standing on a chair in the smoke telling everyone the news. 'Lift your glasses, everyone,' he said proudly. 'To Charlie boy and Mariette.'

As he lifted his Fireball to his lips, the tall, cool Angela shouted, 'And one for him!' There was a great big *bang* under Pop's chair and he went flying back.

Ma, laughing so much she was almost crying, picked him up. Drink all over his face, he had only one thing to say: 'Perfect!'


## CHAPTER NINE

Later, when everybody was gone, Pop and Ma sat in the kitchen laughing about the donkeys and the fireworks. Pop opened a beer and asked Ma if Charlie knew about the baby.

*There was a great big bang under Pop's chair and he went flying back.*

'She's not going to have one now,' Ma said. 'She was just a bit late this month, that's all.'

'Oh . . .?' Pop said. 'Perfect.' He heard rain outside.

'But I'm going to have one,' Ma said.

Pop didn't seem very surprised. 'How did that happen then?'

'How! What do you mean *how*?'

'I mean when.'

'That night we listened to the birds in the forest.'

Pop watched Ma playing with the rings on her sausage-like fingers and had an idea. 'Why don't we get married too, Ma?'

'Why not? I've got to have these rings cut off, haven't I? They're beginning to hurt my fingers again.'

For a minute they were silent. Pop thought about the new baby. Ma thought about what it would be like to be married.

Mr Charlton and Mariette came in from the sitting-room. Pop told them that he was very happy for them and opened a bottle of wine. 'Yes, everything's perfect,' he said, filling glasses for everyone. 'Now, me and Ma have something to tell you.'

The news didn't seem to surprise either Mariette or Mr Charlton. But Mr Charlton started to think. 'Now, wait a minute, Pop,' he said very seriously. 'You mustn't hurry into this.'

'Hurry?' Ma said, and started laughing.

'I mean you must think about taxes. You see, it's cheaper if you're not married. Did you know that?'

'Really?' Pop said. He looked at Ma. 'Oh, well, if it's cheaper, we're happy like this, aren't we, Ma?'

'Good,' Mr Charlton said. 'It'll be better for you when you pay.'

'Pay what?' Pop said, looking uncomfortable.

'Your taxes,' Mr Charlton said. 'You know as well as I do you'll have to pay one day.'

'That's what you think!' Pop said.

'People have eyes, Pop. They notice Rolls-Royces.'

Pop started laughing. 'What, that old car? Someone gave it to me.'

'Sooner or later the Tax Office will get very interested in you.'

'You're not going to go back to that old office, are you?' Ma said.

Mr Charlton didn't seem very sure.

'Yes, it's time you used your head, Charlie,' Pop said. 'There are better things to do than sitting in offices. Look, I'm going to knock a big house down soon. Why don't you help me? We'll keep some of the stones from it and build a nice little house for you and Mariette.'

'Oh, wonderful!' Mariette said, jumping up and throwing her arms round Pop.

'Perfect,' Pop said. He went to the door to watch the rain. Mr Charlton felt it was the right thing to go and stand with him.

'Listen,' Pop said. 'It's just what the fruit needs now.'

Everybody listened to the rain.

'Yes,' Pop said. 'Everything's just perfect.'

# EXERCISES

## Vocabulary Work

Look back at the 'Dictionary Words' in this story. Make sure that you know the meaning of each word.

Try to use the words in sentences. For example, you can use several words in sentences, like this : 'First we picked the strawberries, then we weighed them.'

| | | |
|---|---|---|
| jelly | scrap | to weigh |
| strawberries | tax | breast |
| to pick | cocktail | brassière |
| to earn | to fill | donkey |
| goose | fireworks | race |

Which of these words are living things?

Which words are kinds of food or drink?

Which word is something to wear?

Which word is a part of the body?

Which word means 'useless' or 'unwanted'?

Which word is used with runners and riders?

Which word is the opposite of 'to empty'?

Which two words are used with money?

## Comprehension

*Chapters 1–2*

1 Who are these three people?

  a A young, white-faced man with glasses.

  b A very fat lady who likes eating and cooking.

  c A beautiful young girl who loves riding.

2 Make a list of all the food and drink which the Larkins gave to Mr Charlton. How did he feel at the end of the evening?

*Chapters 3–6*

3 How many people sat down at Sunday dinner in the Larkins' garden? Who were the two visitors?

4 Why was Mariette angry with Pauline Jackson?

5 'Please, please! Another one!' What does Miss Pilchester want Pop Larkin to give her?

*Chapters 7–9*

6 Which of these people won a race?

a the Brigadier

b Mariette

c Miss Pilchester

d Mr Charlton

What kind of race was it?

7 Why is Pop Larkin interested in buying the Bluff-Gores' big house?

8 Pop and Ma Larkin clearly want Mr Charlton and Mariette to get married quickly. Why is this?

9 What are the names of these people?

a A silver-haired woman with very long teeth.

b A woman of about forty years old who wears thick grey clothes and always rides a bicycle.

c A heavy man with a red nose.

d A tall, fair, very beautiful young woman with wonderfully warm eyes.

e A sad-looking man with yellowish skin.

f A tall, straight man who wears old trousers with a hole on the left knee.

g A very pretty, well-built young woman with perfect white teeth.

10 Pop Larkin and the others talk about money and prices at different times in the story. Choose the right answers to the questions

£500     5% of the price     £15     £5     £150

a How much could a large family earn in one day's strawberry-picking?

b How much did Pop pay for his new cocktail cupboard?

c How much does Mr Charlton *guess* that Pop earns in one year?

d How much does Pop *say* he usually earns in one week?

e How much does Lady Bluff-Gore want if she helps Pop to buy her husband's old house?

## Discussion

1 This is a funny story but it also has some serious things to say. What do you think they are?
2 Do you think people live better, more happily, in the country or in the city? Why?
3 Pop Larkin is always giving things to people, helping them, inviting them to meals. Is he just a very kind man or is he really a clever man who wants to get rich and live well?


## Writing

1 Describe everything about a wonderful meal you have eaten. Where did you have it? What did you eat and drink? Who was with you?
2 On page 11, Pop makes a cocktail called a 'Rolls-Royce'. Look at what is in this drink, then describe how to make one of the other cocktails in the book (a Driver, a Snakebite, a Fireball or a Green Spider); or how to make *your* special cocktail (and give your cocktail a name too).
3 Mr Charlton decides not to return to work at the tax office. As Mr Charlton, write a letter to the office to tell them why you are not returning and what you are going to do instead. (150 words)


## Review

1 Who is your favourite person in this story? Why?
2 Did you enjoy this book? Why or why not?